CELEBRATING INCOMPETENT GRADUATE

Dr. Olori Ogheneovo Benjamin

Table of Contents

CHAPTER 1

Fibodi School Days

Amizo is a rural community known to be a harbor of oil wells, coal, diamond, silicon, iron ore, with other natural resources. The leadership of the community is full of incompetency, grid by agitation and protest from the people as a signs of failure in governance to ameliorate the suffering of the people.

The indigenes of Amizo were said to be the first immigrants from the middle east in 1852 as a result of the Crimean war. Since they left their refugee camp to their present abode, they have put up the spirit of resistance against all illss.

Athough, the community has no good roads, no pipe borne water, no hospital but it has primary and secondary schools with cricket holes roof. The people of Amizo dogged some bore holes for themselves and make use of traditional midwives and native doctors as their alternative means for orthodox medicine.

Most of the school teachers comes from the nearest town of Zimba which is about 843 kilometers, they seldom come to work and when they do, they feel very tired and might not be able to go the next day. While they also complaint of poor salary from the government without listening ears.

As a result of the poor educational system in Amizo, Chief Korobia, a retired rubber tapper decided to send his only son, Fibodi to Zimba for college education where he finished with the influence of his father as a known Chief at Amizo.

Fibodi also passed his West African Examination Council, WAEC and National Examination Council, NECO in a prescribed special centres in Zimba metropolis. These centres are also known as A1 and Miracle centres in spite of the poor educational foundation in these areas like Amizo schools.

Almost all the candidates of the schools are products of A1 but they cannot put pen on paper neither make use of computer without waiting for the already made script from the centre managers who helps to destroy the moral, social, psychological and spiritual intelligent of the learners. The schools have produced a lot of clowns who cannot express themselves logically neither be able to analyze ratio in mathematics or nouns as a subject or object from predicates.

Chief Korobia talked to one of his childhood friend who was opportune to be in the University of Washington, now a Professor at Kafio University in Zimba metropolis, to assist his son, Fibodi for admission in spite of the fact that his son did not merit to be admitted due to his failure in the Post Unified Tertiary and Matriculation Examination, UTME conducted by the university.

The chain of help – me – I – will - help - you without regard for merits led Fibodi into Kafio University with high jubilation as soon as Chief Korobia received a phone call from his son that he had gotten his admission letter.

Chief Korobia shutdown the beer palours for whoever that cares to eat and drink any brand of the beer. His wife Chimotikala had also informed their pastors for thanksgiving service which will be coming up next Sunday while invitations where passed to friends and well wishers to join them for the wonderful work of God in their lives and the church was cowed into celebration of people without that lacks integrity.

Fibodi poor performance in school examinations was hinged on lack of dedicated teachers due to poor remuneration, lack of teaching and learning materials and unconducive learning environment which the government is unable to put in place. Teaching and learning in Zimba became worse like the primary and secondary schools experience Fibodi had at Amozi community.

These unavailability of materials for teaching and learning also have bearing in the university system, led the Association of Senior Staff of Universities, ASSU to embark on incessant strike. Eventually, four years course became eight or ten years to become a graduate.

Fibodi and his mates graduated after seven years of been in Kafio University. He graduated with two – one 2:1 from the department of zoology.

CHAPTER 2

BACK to Amizo

Fibodi entered a motorcycle which broke down on his way to the village due to bad roads that vehicles cannot ply. He seeked the help of the villagers who were returning from the farm to carry his luggages to the community.

On his arrival at the village square, many could not recognize him because, he has put a man stature with beard over his face with a dreaded voice. Those that recognizes him rushed at him with jubilation as they accompanied him to his fathers' compound. On sighting his only begotten son, Chief Korobia organized graduation party and set the whole community agog.

The next day, the village Chiefs of Amozi happily organized another party for Fibodi at the community town hall. Fibodi was called upon to address the community on his experience as a graduate and to discuss strategies to ameliorate the suffering of the people as well as to present issues that can draw the attention of governments to their community.

Standing on the podium with a public address system which was donated to the community by a politician from Zimba fifteen years ago, he introduced himself and said; ‘’as you all know, expressing oneself in English language is one of the most difficult task. Even people that studied it as a course in the university also fail it. But I will try my best’’.

Trying to express thoughts further, he said; ‘’you my people, I believe say, una don enjoy the seasonal palm wine that is enough to be exported for exchange for dollars to naira via drinking it all. What else are you people expecting? I studied zoology but I did not see leopard, lion, chimpanzee, crocodile neither antelope in the zoo nor neither in the class. We you blame me? No, blame the government. I am here to present to you that everyone here are in the zoo and can be zoologise as Kambio is concern.’’

Kambio is his nick name as a leader of Marijuana club in kafio University. One of the young lady's asked Fibodi to explain the benefits of zoology to the community and he answered by saying, ''as a matter of policy, I can be arrested if I mention them because of the sense in their names.''

It is obvious that majority of politician from this area cannot speak good English. It seems they have dementia but they will never accept it even when medical doctors and psychologists made them to know about it.

During his address, the guests who clapped for Fibodi after introducing himself, became ashamed, wept like Jesus and left the hall one after the other with sadness. Chief Korobia who thought his son could impress his audience also wept for the waste of his hard earn currency that were enough to feed and train the orphans.

Fibodi left Amizo with shame and disgrace after two days of his shameless address to his people in preparation for his National Youth Service Corp, NYSC.

After the mandatory one year service, Fibodi came back to Amizo, bought food items, clothings and shared to the villagers and promised them that he is the only politician to be, who have the ability to emancipate the people from suffering when he steps into the seat to representative the people in government from Amizo community.

CHAPTER 3

The Election Year

Prior to the elections, Fibodi brought to focus the recruited members of his Marijuana club from Zimba and environs. He gave each member the sum of twenty five thousand naira (#25,000) only. He equally gave guns and ammunitions to some rootless men and named them vigilante and community police with the aid of some renown political sponsors from Zimba metropolis who assured him of done – deal to the position of the representative of the people.

Fibodi promised that; the road to Amizo will be fixed within six months into elective office, underground power supply, modern water board where water will be rushing shhhhhhhhhhhhhhhhh without close and comma. A lot of commissioners will be appointed in my government from Amizo to take care of stomach infrastructure. ''I will empower the youths by making available keke, motorcycle and even buys cars for the ladies. I will buy cutlass, wheelbarrow for agricultural oriented people so that we will have enough cassava to eat in all season.

The people applauded him again ahead of the elections. Fibodi and his pay masters from Zimba never envisage that another person could rise as the representative of the people when Sikebor declared his intention to run for the same office. Though, not educated as such, but Sikebor has school certificate with three credits.

Dr Gianna also emerged from the University of Wale with his doctoral degree and equally put forward his manifestos before the people. Unknown to the people, Fibodi planned to kill, maim and to disfranchise the people through snashing of ballot boxes and voting machines should be case the election did not work in his favour and in order for the election umpire to declare him the winner through the arrangement of the political gurus in

Zimba who are doing underground work to bribe the election umpire. This bring about the high levels of corruption that perverted justice in high places against the poor masses.

CHAPTER 4

Campaign and Manifestos

Beginning with the campaign, Fibodi stood tall with an intrinsic view that he is the only educated person amidst the contestants. He promised heaven and earth as he planned to build international airport, seaport, bridges, free food for all, free school fees and he equally promised the people the types of road net – work in the United Kingdom, United State of America and Australia which he saw in the pictures and television. He further promised to built a zoological garden of Eden where he will re – name all the animals like Adam did and made the people to understand that his wife will be the first lady who will ventilate issues across women.

He promised to replicate the types of hospitals in India, China and Israel. He promised to buy motorcade that has cold – room to transport dead bodies to enable them gets to their ancestral homes.

He promised to changed the air we breath to an angelic atmosphere and promised a paradise on earth where angels will visit from heaven and report to God through Mary. He almost promised raising the dead. And the people applauded him.

The second contestant, Mr Sikebor climbed the podium and hailed the people for their hard – work over the centuries without given up on agriculture and promise to revamp the agricultural sector and promised to get fishing net for the people as well as to tarred all the roads.

In the manifestos of the most highly educated person in their midst, Dr Gianna, the great grand son of Aminose whose parents worked in Western Rice Mill in the United States of America, is in the race too. He was not only sent to one of the best university in the world but he was also trained morally, socially, psychologically and spiritually. Dr Gianna obtained first degree in Philosophy and Human Resources Management (Hon.), Master degree in Material Management and Master in Business Management respectively. Before Dr Gianna proceeded for his Doctoral degree in Economics and Human Capital Management, he taught as a lecturer two in Harvard, Oxford, Cambridge and worked as a consultant for various organizations until he became the Head of various Chartered Management Bodies, organizing conferences for World Health Organisation, WHO and United Nations Trust Fund, UNTF. With his experience as someone whom have worked diligently, competently, and humbly with the best of his ability to elevate the status of those organizations.

Dr. Gianna curriculum vitae is first to none. He's campaign promises put the face of corrupt politicians down as he promised to eradicate corruption through the independent of the Economic and Financial Crime Commission, EFCC, establishment of companies that could produce all that we needed to avoid more of importation but export of goods. His words bring hope and advancement of his community through the revitalization of the education sector, justice system, agricultural sector and foreign investment and linkages.

25th February was fixed for the elections. Fibodi brought a grader (Caterpillar) to fill the bad roads with sand and this will enable the heavy weight politicians from Zimba to drive into Amizo with their heavy duty cars on siren on election day and to convince the people to vote for him.

CHAPTER 5

Typically, this is an era where politicians buys results and certificates forgery are the order of the day and undetected. Except their political opponents whose certificate is genuine that usually investigate their rivals to pull them down through legal communication to the Economic and Financial Crime Commission, EFCC or through the court of law.

The multiplicity of certificates saga are rocking the media and legal air. Dubious journalists are smiling home on daily bases with their brown envelops as a result of covering societal ills while they uncover the stories of those lesser bidder. Magistrates and chief judges are more worrisome as they take turns to swallow constituencies funds stolen by politicians through court cases.

Fibodi is claimed to have also graduated from University of Toronto because of the school international repute. At one point, he claimed to have gotten his West African Examination Certificate in 1968 whereas he presented 1992 certificate to the election umpire with his date of birth bearing the same 1968. Probably, he finished his O' Level the same year he was given birth to.

With these inconsistency, his political rival took him to court and won. Fibodi fought hard and sue for Higher Courts with display of hard currencies before the judges which saw him as the winner at the Apex Court.

Security chiefs are eating so fat for aiding crises in the land. The rich no longer obey Court Order neither obeys the constitution of the land. Fibodi is among those who have no feelings for the masses.

Fibodi eventually became the representative of the people against their yelling's. The excessive loan he took from Zimba politicians has bought him the position of representative of the people and he has to pay back through subvention from government which is primarily met for constituency projects. His promises on developments has hit the rock as the political godfathers are strangulating financially on the annual budget in order for them to get back their invested funds. For four years, Fibodi could not achieve any of his set goals and resorted to blackmail while guarding himself with heavy armed policemen and soldiers with the fear of been mobbed by the people of Amizo and environ.

CHAPTER 6

At this time, the church has become a harbor place for Fibodi and his political gangsters. The church offers the politicians the front seats without questioning them on their failure to the entire community because they donates heavily to the churches and buy expensive cars for the pastors.

The pastors on their parts keeps extorting the poor in the word ''give and it shall be given unto you'', happy are the givers than the receivers''. They emphasis on tilting as if it is the only commandment in the Holy Scriptures. Nobody question them because the churches registered on non – tax payment purview of Cooperate Affairs Commission, CAC.

Although, the church gives few scholarships to the children of the rich.

www.ingramcontent.com/pod-product-compliance
Lightning Source LLC
LaVergne TN
LVHW052116160826
845678LV00015B/3591

* 9 7 9 8 3 7 1 4 5 4 7 2 0 *